W9-BIH-304

DATE DUE

Soldiers of the Civil War

Diane Smolinski

Series Consultant:
Lieutenant Colonel G.A. LoFaro

Heinemann Library
Chicago, Illinois

© 2001 Reed Educational & Professional Publishing
Published by Heinemann Library,
an imprint of Reed Educational & Professional Publishing,
Chicago, IL
Customer Service 888-454-2279
Visit our website at www.heinemannlibrary.com

Designed by Herman Adler Design
Printed in Hong Kong

05 04 03 02 01
10 9 8 7 6 5 4 3 2 1

Library of Congress Cataloging-in-Publication Data

Smolinski, Diane, 1950-
  Soldiers of the Civil War / Diane Smolinski.
    p. cm. -- (Americans at war. Civil War)
  Includes bibliographical references and index.
    ISBN 1-58810-098-7
  1. United States. Army--History--Civil War, 1861-1865-
Juvenile literature. 2. Confederate States of America.
Army--History--Juvenile literature. 3. United States.
Army--Military life--History--19th century--Juvenile
literature. 4. Confederate States of America.
Army--Military life--Juvenile literature. 5. Soldiers--United
States--History--19th century--Juvenile literature. 6.
Soldiers--United States--Social conditions--19th century-
Juvenile literature. 7. United States--History--Civil War,
1861-1865--Social aspects--Juvenile literature. 8. Lee,
Robert E. (Robert Edward), 1807-1870--Juvenile literature.
9. Grant, Ulysses S. (Ulysses Simpson), 1822-1885-
Juvenile literature. [1. Soldiers--History--19th century.
2. United States--History--Civil War, 1861-1865.]
I. Title.
E607 .S66 2002
973.7--dc21
                                    00-012395

Acknowledgments
The author and publishers are grateful to the following for
permission to reproduce copyright material: p.3 Illinois State
Historical Library; p.4, 7 inset, 17 top, 20–21, 25 top Chicago
Historical Society; p.5A State Historical Society of Wisconsin;
p.5B, 22–23, 24–25, 25 inset Corbis; p.6-7, 9 bottom, 10
bottom, 11 top, 12 top, 12 bottom, 14–15, 26 National
Archives; p.6 inset Collection of Don Troiani; p.8 top, 8 bottom
left, 8 bottom right, 10, 15 inset, 16, 23 top Library of
Congress; p.9 top N/A/Archive Photos/PictureQuest; p.11
bottom Don Troiani; p.13 Bettmann/Corbis; p.14 inset
Medford Historical Society/Corbis; p.17 bottom Ohio State
Historical Society; p.18 top Courtesy of Eddy and Becky
Davenport; p.18–19 Rochester Museum and Science Center;
p.19 inset Library of Virginia; p.20 Archive
Photos/PictureQuest; p.24 top Courtesy of Mr. Edward Boots;
p.29 inset Museum of American History/Smithsonian
Institution; p.29 Medford Historical Society Collection/Corbis.

Cover photograph courtesy of Library of Congress.

About the Author
Diane Smolinski is a teacher for the Seminole County School
District in Florida. She earned B.S. of Education degrees
from Duquesne University and Slippery Rock University in
Pennsylvania. For the past fourteen years, Diane has taught
the Civil War curriculum to fourth and fifth graders. She was
also instrumental in writing the pioneer room curriculum,
indicative of the Civil War era, for the school district's
student history museum. Diane lives with her husband,
two daughters, and a cat.

Special Thanks to Mr. Edward Boots and to Eddy and Becky
Davenport for their generosity in supplying materials and
for their interest and enthusiasm in this project.

About the Consultant
G.A. LoFaro is a lieutenant colonel in the U.S. Army currently
stationed at Fort McPherson, Georgia. After graduating from
West Point, he was commissioned in the infantry. He has
served in a variety of positions in the 82nd Airborne Division,
the Ranger Training Brigade, and Second Infantry Division
in Korea. He has a Masters Degree in U.S. History from the
University of Michigan and is completing his Ph.D in U.S.
History at the State University of New York at Stony Brook.
He has also served six years on the West Point faculty where
he taught military history to cadets.

Some words are shown in bold, **like this.** You can
find out what they mean by looking in the glossary.

Contents

A Call to Arms!

Fighting to Protect the Union

In 1861, the main goal of the Union, or the North, was to reunite the states as one nation. The North had the manpower, industrial capabilities, money, and available resources to do it. Leaders in the North believed they could easily win this war.

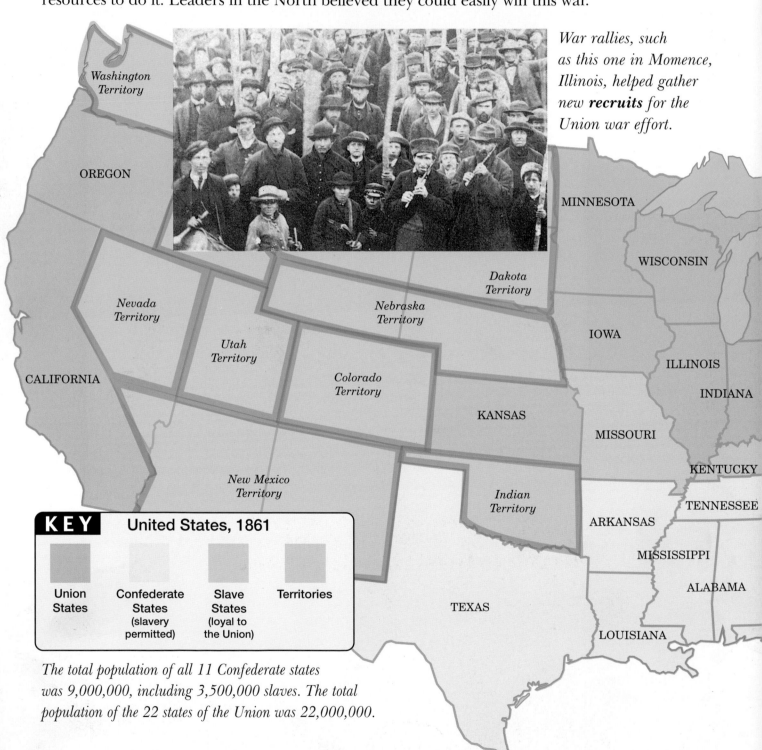

*War rallies, such as this one in Momence, Illinois, helped gather new **recruits** for the Union war effort.*

KEY — United States, 1861

Union States	Confederate States (slavery permitted)	Slave States (loyal to the Union)	Territories

The total population of all 11 Confederate states was 9,000,000, including 3,500,000 slaves. The total population of the 22 states of the Union was 22,000,000.

4

Fighting to Protect States Rights

In 1861, the main goal of the Confederacy, or the South, was to preserve the southern way of life, which included the right to own slaves. The southern states **seceded** to form a separate country called the Confederate States of America. Southern leaders were certain their superior military leadership would overcome the North's advantages of manpower and resources. These leaders believed they could win this war.

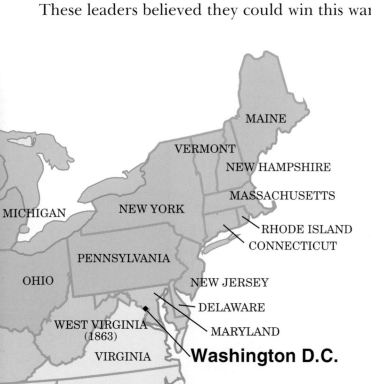

*At the beginning of the war, men in the North and South hurried to **enlistment** offices to join in the excitement of war.*

Organizing Armies

Once the southern states **seceded,** leaders in the North and South asked citizens to volunteer for military duty. No one imagined how deeply and permanently this conflict would scar the nation.

In the North

- The Union already had an organized army. But leaders needed to **recruit,** and later **draft,** many more soldiers to fight the war.

- The Union Army had **commissioned** officers. As the size of the army grew, more officers were commissioned.

- Male citizens could join the Union Army. They could **enlist** for three months to three years.

- On March 3, 1863, the U.S. Congress passed a law that started conscription, or a draft system. The law required that men between the ages of 20 and 45 be enrolled in a state **militia** and be available when needed.

According to the U.S. War Department, more than 2,898,304 men were enlisted in the Union Army throughout the war. It is estimated that 600,000 to more than 1,000,000 men were enlisted in the Confederate Army. The southern states did not always keep accurate records, so only estimates can be made.

In the South

- The Confederacy had individual state militias that were later organized into several larger armies. They needed to recruit large numbers of men.

- Some officers resigned their commissions in the U.S. Army to join the Confederate Army. As the size of the armies grew, more officers were commissioned.

- White male citizens could join the Confederate Army. They could enlist for up to three years.

- On April 16, 1862, the southern Congress passed the first National Conscription Act for males aged 18 to 35. Everyone would serve for three years. In September 1862, the age limit was extended from 18 to 45 years. In February 1864, the age limits were changed again to include men aged 17 to 50.

MY FELLOW-CITIZENS, TO ARMS!

I have just received a message direct from the highest authority in the Confederacy, to call upon the Militia Organizations to come forth, and upon all other Citizens to organize Companies for the defence of this City against immediate attack of the enemy. They are approaching, and you may have to meet them before Monday morning. I can do no more than give you this warning of their near approach.

REMEMBER NEW ORLEANS!

Richmond is now in your hands. Let it not fall under the rule of another BUTLER. Rally, then, to your Officers to-morrow morning at 10 o'clock, on BROAD STREET, in front of the CITY HALL.

JOSEPH MAYO,
Mayor of Richmond.

Saturday Afternoon, June 27, 1863.

Soldiers of the Civil War

Civil War Officers

More than 1,000 officers served as generals in the Civil War. Some went to military schools such as West Point, Virginia Military Institute, and the Citadel and were commissioned upon graduation. Some leading citizens organized groups of men to enlist and were appointed officers of these units.

Two Professional Soldiers

U.S. Army officers who wanted to join the Confederate Army had to resign their commissions in the U. S. Army and then join the Confederate Army. Two famous Civil War generals graduated from the United States Military Academy at West Point, fought in the Mexican War, and were skilled leaders. Robert E. Lee fought for the Confederacy, while Ulysses S. Grant fought for the Union.

General (Hiram) Ulysses S. Grant 1822–1885

Education and Training

- Grant attended school in Georgetown, Ohio. He was a good math student and liked to ride horses in his spare time.
- Grant attended college at the U.S. Military Academy at West Point, graduating in 1843.

Experience

- Grant served in the Mexican War as a **quartermaster.**
- After finishing his first commitment in the U.S. Army, Grant resigned and returned to Missouri to farm. Later he moved his family to Galena, Illinois, to work in his father's store.

Grant

1820	1830	1840

1807 Lee is born

1822 Grant is born
1829 Lee graduates from West Point

Lee

1843 Grant graduates from West Point
1846 Lee and Grant both are sent to Texas to fight in the Mexican War

Grant

General Robert Edward Lee 1807–1870

Lee

Education and Training

- Lee attended school in Alexandria, Virginia. He worked hard and was a good student.
- Lee attended college at the U.S. Military Academy at West Point, graduating in 1829.

Experience

- Lee served in the Mexican War. He was an engineering officer who helped build gun **batteries.**
- Lee stayed in the U.S. Army, serving in the **cavalry** in Texas. Later, he was appointed Superintendent of West Point.

General Grant, (standing, third from right) was usually surrounded by his staff and advisers.

1850	1860	1870	1880
1852 Lee becomes Superintendent of West Point **1854** Grant resigns from the U.S. Army	**1861** Grant rejoins the U.S. Army Lee resigns from the U.S. Army and joins the Confederate Army **1862** Lee becomes the commander of the Confederate forces in Virginia **1864** Grant becomes the commander of all the U.S. armies **1865** Lee becomes the commander of all the Confederate armies **1868** Grant is elected president of the U.S.	**1870** Lee dies **1872** Grant elected to second term as U.S. president	**1885** Grant dies

Grant

Grant: The War and After

Civil War Years

- Grant rejoined the Union Army in 1861 as a colonel of the 21st Illinois **Infantry regiment.**
- Grant became the general in charge of all the Union armies in 1864.
- Grant was an accomplished horseman. His favorite horse was named Cincinnati.

After the War

- Grant remained the head of the Union Army.
- Grant was elected president of the United States in 1868 and again in 1872.

Even though General Grant was an intense and determined fighter, he would not allow Union soldiers to ridicule the enemy after the surrender at Appomattox. He stated, "The war is over, the **Rebels** are again our countrymen."

Grant outside his tent near Cold Harbor, Virginia.

Lee: The War and After

Civil War Years

- General Winfield Scott, General-in-Chief of the Union Army, offered Lee a command in the U.S. Army. However, when Virginia **seceded,** Lee went home to fight for the Confederacy.

- For most of the war, Lee commanded the Confederate Army of Northern Virginia. Near the end of the war, he became commander of all Confederate armies.

- Five horses traveled with Lee throughout the war, but Traveller was his favorite. He rode Traveller to the surrender at Appomattox.

Lee

After the War

- Lee became president of Washington College in Virginia. Today, it is named Washington and Lee College. Lee is buried on the college grounds.

- Lee could not hold a public office after the war because his U.S. citizenship was taken away as part of his surrender.

General Lee was a master military leader, a gentleman, and a beloved hero. His daughter Mary remarked, "What a name and inheritance he has left his children."

Lee was well versed in military tactics, and was a strong leader on the battlefield.

Enlisted Soldiers

Men from all walks of life **enlisted** in the Union and Confederate armies. New soldiers often received only basic military training before going into battle. But regardless of experience, men on both sides fought with great courage during the four-year-long Civil War.

Union Enlisted Soldiers

- Union soldiers were nicknamed "Billy Yanks" or "Yankees."

- Union soldiers usually had enough food because the Union had reliable transportation systems by which to bring it to them. Hardtack was a hard cracker given to Union soldiers preparing for battle.

- Union enlisted soldiers were paid $13 each month.

Union soldiers, such as these members of the 93rd New York Infantry, generally gathered in small groups for meals.

Confederate Enlisted Soldiers

- Confederate soldiers were nicknamed "Johnny Rebs" or "Rebels."

- Providing food for Confederate soldiers was difficult. Soldiers often ate food that was growing nearby. As battles were mostly fought in Confederate states, crops and livestock were eaten by both armies or were damaged in battle. Poor transportation systems made shipping food difficult. Cornbread, or "pone," was a type of biscuit or pancake often given to Confederate soldiers.

- Confederate enlisted soldiers were paid $11 each month.

The average age of a soldier in either army was 25. Most soldiers were about 5 feet 8 inches tall (1.7 meters) and weighed about 143 pounds (65 kilograms). Some boys as young as nine years old served as musicians and performed other jobs, such as carrying water and helping cooks and doctors. Some of these boys saw combat and died fighting for their cause.

Most men were placed in **infantry** units, some were assigned to **cavalry** units, and others were trained to fire and maintain the **artillery.**

Infantry

Most soldiers in both armies served in the **infantry.** Infantrymen marched from battle to battle. If they needed to travel long distances, they sometimes went by train or boat. In battle, infantrymen had to attack on foot, often fighting hand to hand, and then defend a position against enemy attacks.

Equipment was essential for the infantryman to survive. Northern industry provided Union infantrymen with plenty of items, such as uniforms, boots, blankets, eating utensils, canteens, cartridge boxes, tents, weapons, and **haversacks.** Union infantrymen were better equipped, had more food, and greatly outnumbered the Confederate infantry.

Confederate infantry soldiers were often given only a portion of the supplies they needed. They brought supplies and muskets from home.

The basic weapon for Union and Confederate infantrymen was a musket, such as this Union soldier is holding. Firing one shot at a time, an infantryman could load and fire up to three shots each minute.

Field Artillery

Men in both armies were trained to fire and maintain cannons on wheels called **artillery.** The men, cannons, equipment, and horses needed to transport the equipment were called a **battery.**

Horse-drawn field artillery could go into battle with the infantry or **cavalry.** It shelled the opposing army hiding in **trenches** or behind **fortifications.** Field artillery was also important to the army being attacked. Cannons could destroy large numbers of attacking troops moving across open ground. Artillery fire also protected retreating troops as they escaped.

Heavy artillery was pulled by larger teams of horses. These batteries were placed at the rear of the army because they were designed to fire long distances. Heavy artillery was used to destroy important targets, such as bridges, railroads, or forts. The disadvantage to it was that it could not be moved quickly.

A Confederate soldier stands at attention.

Artillerymen, such as these from Battery D of the Second U.S. Artillery, were responsible for preparing the cannons for battles.

Calvary

Mounted on horses, carrying firearms and swords, the **cavalry** in both armies served many important purposes. Cavalry units were the "eyes and ears" of the armies. Scouting ahead of the **infantry** and **artillery,** these units gathered information about the opposing army's location, number of soldiers, and readiness.

By meeting the enemy first, the cavalry slowed down the opposing army, giving the attacking army a chance to organize an attack or set up a defense. If troops had to retreat, the cavalry delayed the enemy, allowing the infantry and artillery to move to a safe position.

Cavalry troopers scouted ahead for the best roads for the armies to travel, looked for food, located places to cross rivers, and held these places until the main force of the army arrived safely.

African American Soldiers

During the war, nearly 180,000 African Americans fought for the Union Army. Thirteen of these soldiers were awarded the Medal of Honor.

In the Union Army

- At first, African Americans were not welcome as soldiers. Negro units, as they were called during this time period, were formed when **enlistment** times had run out and casualties had reduced the size of the Union Army.
- Negro units were usually infantry units.
- For most of the war, African Americans received less pay than white soldiers.

In the Confederate Army

- Slaves were not allowed to be soldiers because they were not considered citizens. Near the end of the war, when the Confederacy was desperate, some African-American units were formed, but these never saw combat.
- Most drove supply wagons, were cooks, or helped in the hospitals.
- Many Confederate officers brought their slaves with them while with the army.

African-American soldiers joined the Union Army to help fight to end slavery.

One Confederate Volunteer

On May 14, 1862, in Montgomery, Alabama, John Forbes Davenport **enlisted** in the Confederate Army for three years or until the end of the war. He wrote many letters to his wife and children during the war.

Writing letters was the only form of communication most Confederate soldiers had with their families. Davenport's letters show what he saw, felt, and thought as he traveled through the camps and battlefields of the South.

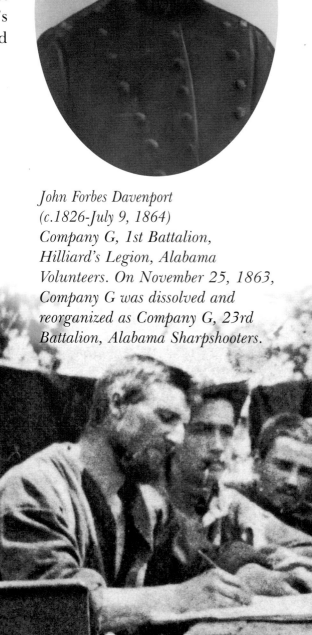

John Forbes Davenport (c.1826–July 9, 1864) Company G, 1st Battalion, Hilliard's Legion, Alabama Volunteers. On November 25, 1863, Company G was dissolved and reorganized as Company G, 23rd Battalion, Alabama Sharpshooters.

Life in the army was very different from life at home. Soldiers missed their families, food was scarce, and Confederate money was nearly worthless. Davenport spent over a month's wages on food in a matter of days. Soldiers often had to eat crops growing in the fields. Salt in their diets helped prevent **scurvy.** The Confederate Army was often short of equipment as well as food. Soldiers captured clothing or weapons from Union soldiers to get the supplies they needed.

Formal schooling was not always necessary for the common citizen in the 1800s. Words were often spelled as they would have been pronounced, and little punctuation was used.

September the 7, 1862 – Cumblin Gap
My Dear Wife. you dont know how glad my heart would be if I could see you and them little jewels that haven in mercy has given us...I spent 15 dollars for something to eat on the march...after we got here we lived on **rostingyears** almost entirely without salt...I came on one of their lieutenants... in the rostingyear field. I took my old big knife with me...I made a dash at him...he run thru the corn...He dropped his coat...his pickets opened fire on me. I stopped to get his coat and my **haversack** of rostingyears before I left...

Hiring a substitute to take the place of a drafted soldier was common at this time, but it was considered unpatriotic on the part of the soldier being replaced.

Conscripted soldiers in both armies who did not wish to fight paid undrafted men to enlist in their place.

This Febuary the 2. 1863
My Dear Wife... You should recieve seventy too dollars and thirty three cents per month. Solgers waiges is onley eleven dollars per month...let me know whither he payes you or not. I am determend he shall pay acorden to contract...

SUBSTITUTE NOTICES.

WANTED—A SUBSTITUTE. Apply at No. 38 Linwood House, Main street, between the Spotswood and American Hotels, same side of the street, between 9 and 10 o'clock A. M. Any citizen of the Confederate States, over 35 years old, may come. A Kentuckian preferred. No forieger need apply.
jy 8—2t*

WANTED—A SUBSTITUTE.—I will pay the sum of $1,000, cash, for a SUBSTITUTE, to serve in Company K, 3d Alabama regiment, for two years, or the war. Good references required. Apply to "A.," at this office, between the hours of 9 and 10 A. M., or 4 and 5 P. M.
jy 8—3t*

WANTED—A SUBSTITUTE.—None need come unless a *citizen* of the Confederate States, over 35 years of age. Such a one would do well by applying between 7 and 12 o'clock TO-DAY, at 75 Ballard House.
jy 8—1t*

WANTED—By a young man, of good character, a place as SUBSTITUTE; exempt by age. He can be seen at No. 51 American Hotel, or will receive communications addressed to "J. J.," through Richmond P. O.
jy 8—3t*

WANTED—A SUBSTITUTE—To go into the infantry service. A liberal price will be given by applying at No. 132 Main street, for the next two days. [jy 8—2t*] W. A T.

WANTED—A SUBSTITUTE for the war. A Marylander preferred. Apply at Wm. H. Yeatman's shop, on 8th street, between Grace and Franklin.
jy 8—1t*

SUBSTITUTE.—Wanted, a SUBSTITUTE for the war. Apply for "J. H.," at the Dispatch office, between 9 and 11 o'clock, corner Main and 13th streets.
jy 8—2t*

WANTED—Two SUBSTITUTES—To go in for the war. None but non-conscripts need apply, on South side. 12th between Main and Bank streets.
jy 8—5t

WANTED—A SUBSTITUTE.—Address "Box 169," stating where applicant can be seen.
jy 8—2t*

WANTED—A SUBSTITUTE

More than 200,000 Confederate soldiers died during the Civil War. Including those in prisons, it is estimated that disease and sickness killed more than 100,000 of these soldiers.

Confederate soldiers fought to keep life in the South as it was. Once soldiers experienced the horrors of war, they became concerned about other family members volunteering. They wanted to shelter them from the many hardships they had seen. But even though soldiers lived in danger, they understood the enthusiasm of other family members who also wished to fight for their country.

*This picture of the men of the 1st Virginia **Militia** was taken a few weeks after the fall of Fort Sumter.*

This April the 8. 1863—Lee Springs, Grainger Co East Tenn
My Dearley Beloved Wife...sickness at this time...is verry fatel. Last weeak we burried too of our companey. Tha was...young men in fine helth. ... Boath with newmoney.

May the 1. 1863
Beens Station E. Tennessee
My Dearley Beloved Wife and Children....what plesure it will be...to know that I did helpe to astablish this land of freedom to leave it as a inheritance for my children to enjoy...tell brother Hamel if he is not subject to **conscription** I would rather he would remaining at home...I have seen so much sickness hardships and deths in camp...But if he is subject to conscription or if he is determend to enter the servis I would be glad to have him with me...

Most men **enlisted** in their hometowns with friends and family. Enlisted soldiers saw their friends get wounded or killed and watched commanding officers risk their lives for the cause. During battle, officers often rode horses through the ranks of infantrymen and **artillery.**

As Davenport makes clear in his letters, even though the Union, or "Yankees" as they were often called, had superior **arms,** that alone did not guarantee victory.

Chattnooga Tenn.
Sept 26. 1863
My Dear Wife...tha was armed with the best revolving riffle five shooter... I fired 37 rounds and tuck good ame...the ded yankeys lay in heeps before us...we encamped on the battlefield too nites we would drag the dead yankeys out of our way to...ley down to sleep...

Camp Near Chattanooga
This September the 30. 1863
My Dear Wife and Children...the crye of the wounded was anuf to melt the heart... I could not sleepe...our companey went into the fight with 29 men and caim out with onley 8 men. The 1 Battalion went into the fight with too hundred forty men and caim out with onley fifty men...total loss of our **Brigade** is about 800 men in killed wounded and missing...General Gracey flue from wing to wing between the fire of both armeys giving comand...He had too horses killd under him and meney meney shot went throu his clothing. I had seven shot in throu my coat but non more than grained the skin.

Soldiers on both sides of the conflict dealt with the hardships of war as well as they could. Religious services were held wherever the men camped, most often without a proper clergyman. Soldiers used the nighttime to rest, eat, and resupply their ammunition. It was not practical to fight in the dark, for they could not see the enemy. Prisoners were held, exchanged for other prisoners, or sent to prison camps. Soldiers were buried on or near the fields where they fought. Fighting continued around them. After four years, men on both sides were tired of fighting.

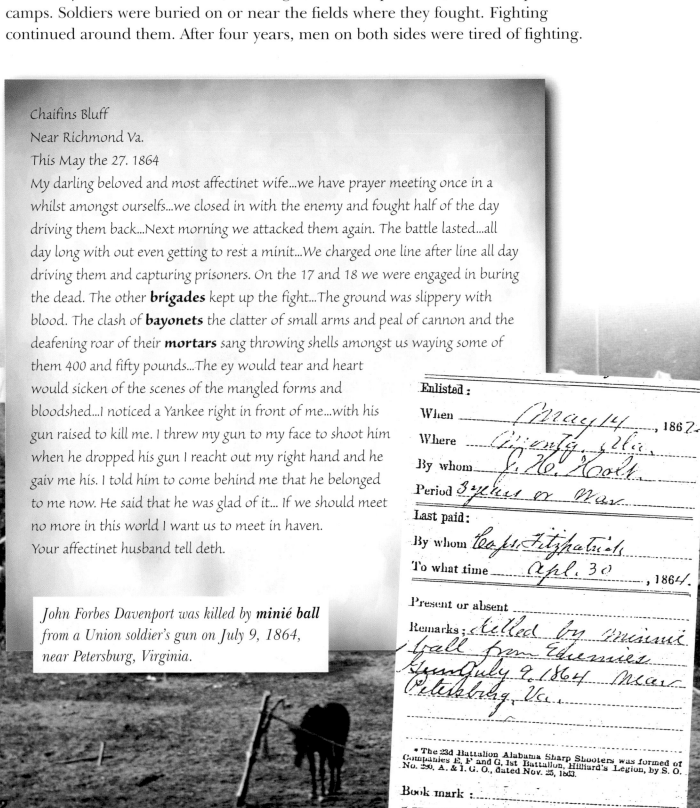

Chaifins Bluff

Near Richmond Va.

This May the 27. 1864

My darling beloved and most affectinet wife...we have prayer meeting once in a whilst amongst ourselfs...we closed in with the enemy and fought half of the day driving them back...Next morning we attacked them again. The battle lasted...all day long with out even getting to rest a minit...We charged one line after line all day driving them and capturing prisoners. On the 17 and 18 we were engaged in buring the dead. The other **brigades** kept up the fight...The ground was slippery with blood. The clash of **bayonets** the clatter of small arms and peal of cannon and the deafening roar of their **mortars** sang throwing shells amongst us waying some of them 400 and fifty pounds...The ey would tear and heart would sicken of the scenes of the mangled forms and bloodshed...I noticed a Yankee right in front of me...with his gun raised to kill me. I threw my gun to my face to shoot him when he dropped his gun I reacht out my right hand and he gaiv me his. I told him to come behind me that he belonged to me now. He said that he was glad of it... If we should meet no more in this world I want us to meet in haven.

Your affectinet husband tell deth.

*John Forbes Davenport was killed by **minié ball** from a Union soldier's gun on July 9, 1864, near Petersburg, Virginia.*

Enlisted :

When _____ May 14 _____, 186 2

Where _____ County, Ala.

By whom _____ G. H. Holt

Period _3 years or War_

Last paid :

By whom _Capt. Fitzpatrick_

To what time _____ Apl. 30 _____, 1864.

Present or absent _____

Remarks : _killed by minnie ball from Enemies gun July 9, 1864 near Petersburg, Va._

* The 23d Battalion Alabama Sharp Shooters was formed of Companies E, F and G, 1st Battalion, Hilliard's Legion, by S. O. No. 290, A. & I. G. O., dated Nov. 25, 1863.

Book mark : _____

Doctors were in great demand during the war. They did their best to attend to wounded soldiers between battles. Here, wounded Confederate soldiers in the Fourteenth Indiana Infantry are treated after the Battle of Antietam.

In the Civil War prison camp pictured below, Confederate prisoners are being guarded by Union soldiers.

One Union Volunteer

Edward Nicholas Boots's letters describe his daily life as a Union infantry soldier. Mr. Boots was a schoolteacher when the war began. His spelling and grammar skills were more refined than those of many soldiers.

Like their Confederate enemies, Union soldiers also slept in open fields. And although both Union and Confederate troops usually marched from place to place, Union soldiers had better access to steamers, or boats, which could move troops longer distances more quickly.

Edward Nicholas Boots (1834–September 1864) 101st Pennsylvania Volunteer Infantry Edward and two cousins enlisted in the Union Army on October 4, 1861, in Beaver County, Pennsylvania.

Soldiers in the Union Army rest after a drilling exercise.

April 1st (1862) on board the Steamer State of Maine, near the entrance of the Potomac river into chesapeak bay
Dear Mother
... we arrived at 11 O'clock at night. We marched into an open field rolled ourselves in our blankets and lay down on the ground until morning...it began to snow hard...got a couple of tents...but the ground was a perfect swamp the boys carried in brush and leaves and spread their blankets on them, about 10 O'clock at night orders were given us to be ready to march in the morning. When we got up it was still raining but we packed up and marched...to embark on board steamers...there are about fifteen hundred troops on board...we are pretty well crowded...

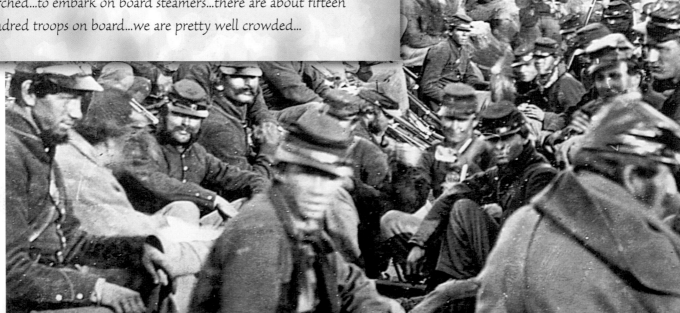

Soldiers endured hardships even when they were not fighting. Bad weather created poor living conditions. These conditions contributed to sickness and disease among the troops.

Camp sixteen miles from Richmond

May 20th (1862)

Dear Mother

...We have marched more than fifty miles in the last two weeks...through heavy rains, laid out at night with no shelter and the rain pouring all the time...

If they were marching through a marshy area, troops often had to build bridges as they went.

Leaders of the North thought it was necessary to capture the Confederate capital city of Richmond, Virginia, to end the war. As it advanced on Richmond, the Union Army used hot air balloons as lookout posts to locate the Confederate Army.

A hot air balloon was used by the Union Army to observe the Battle of Fair Oaks.

Camp on the Chickahominy river on the road to Fort Darling

June 9th (1862)

Dear Mother

Our **Pickets** are close enough to Richmond now to see the spires of buildings in the city...balloon ascensions...give to McClelland all the necessary information about the whereabouts of the rebel army...

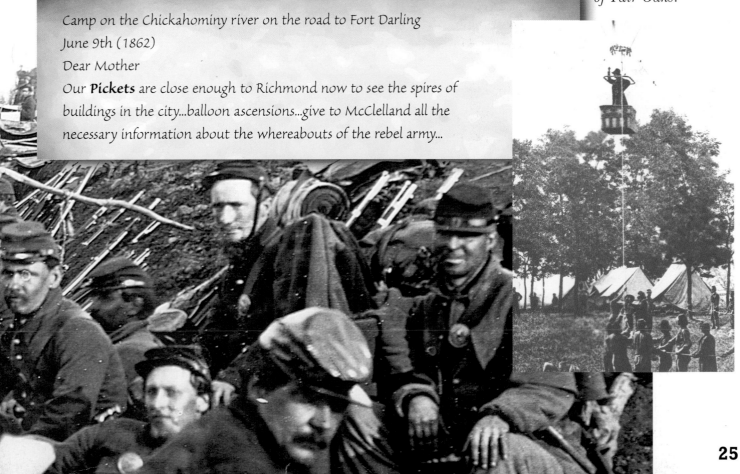

After two years of heavy fighting, families that had soldiers in the army were concerned that **draft** laws would place yet more family members in danger.

Camp 101st Regt P.V. Newbern. N Carolina.

St Patrick's day March 17th (1863)

Dearest Mother,

...You kneed not be uneasy about the draft. The law for the new draft says that when two of a family are already in the army, Two are to be exempt & left at home. You have only two grown up sons at home so they must be exempt.

Sickness killed many soldiers. Nearly 250,000 Union soldiers died from sickness, disease, or accident. Since the armies did not fight much during winter months, soldiers built more permanent log cabins rather than stay in tents. African Americans fled southern states to escape slavery. Some whites fled to avoid conscription laws.

Plymouth N.C.

Oct 11th (1863)

Dear Mother

...the sickness is still very bad & they had two hundred & forty sick one day this week...many fresh graves have been dug since we came....we are crowded with refugees coming within our lines to escape. black as well as white are flying....Winter quarters are being built...We shall soon have a small town of log huts...

It was difficult to deliver mail to troops that were constantly moving. In fact, it was often hard for the army to keep track of its soldiers. During battle, soldiers often were separated from their units and became part of another unit. It took time for the army to find these soldiers, change their records, and then deliver their mail. Soldiers who were sick and unable to march were left behind to defend towns while the rest of their unit went off to battle.

As the war dragged on, fewer men **enlisted.** Some northern units were made up of newly arrived immigrants. The government offered bounties, or bonuses, to attract men to be soldiers.

At the beginning of the war, both sides agreed to release or exchange prisoners within ten days of their capture. Later in the war, this agreement broke down. Prison camps became more common.

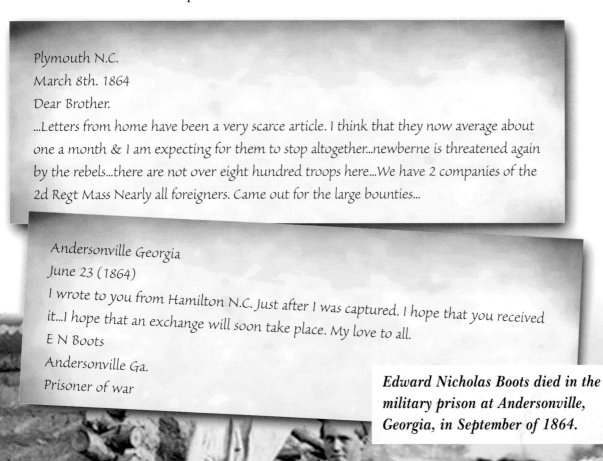

Plymouth N.C.
March 8th. 1864
Dear Brother.
...Letters from home have been a very scarce article. I think that they now average about one a month & I am expecting for them to stop altogether...newberne is threatened again by the rebels...there are not over eight hundred troops here...We have 2 companies of the 2d Regt Mass Nearly all foreigners. Came out for the large bounties...

Andersonville Georgia
June 23 (1864)
I wrote to you from Hamilton N.C. Just after I was captured. I hope that you received it...I hope that an exchange will soon take place. My love to all.
E N Boots
Andersonville Ga.
Prisoner of war

Edward Nicholas Boots died in the military prison at Andersonville, Georgia, in September of 1864.

Civil War Navies

The South could never defeat the North by sheer strength alone. Instead, Southern leaders used their imaginations to invent weapons, including new naval weapons. Although these weapons did not always work perfectly, they gave the South a better chance of defending itself against a much larger Union Navy.

The Union Navy

- In 1861, the Union had 42 wooden sailing vessels.
- The Union had the facilities and materials needed to build many ships. Northern shipbuilders soon built several **ironclads,** river gunboats, and troop transport boats.

The Confederate Navy

- In 1861, the Confederates needed to build a navy. When the southern states **seceded**, they captured some U.S. Navy boats.
- The South had fewer facilities and materials to build ships. They were the first, though, to put an ironclad ship in battle as well as being the first to develop the underwater torpedo and the attack submarine.

War ships in the Union Navy were well-stocked with troops and arms. It was difficult for the Confederate Navy to match their strength.

Conclusion

The fighting spirit of the individual soldier did much to determine the outcome of each battle. This fighting spirit, combined with leadership, technology, weapons, and the economy decided the outcome of the war.

"...we highly resolve that these dead shall not have died in vain..."

From The Gettysburg Address by Abraham Lincoln
November 19, 1863

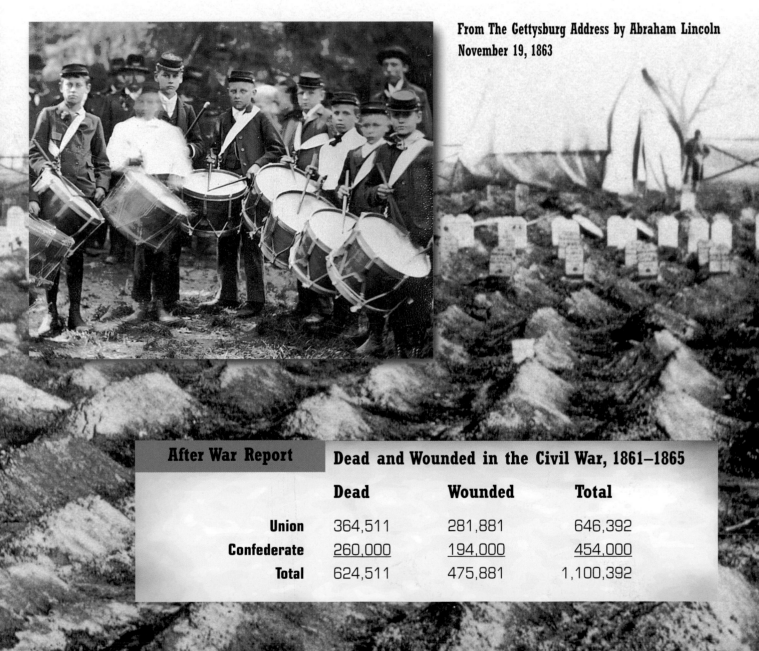

After War Report	Dead and Wounded in the Civil War, 1861–1865		
	Dead	Wounded	Total
Union	364,511	281,881	646,392
Confederate	260,000	194,000	454,000
Total	624,511	475,881	1,100,392

Glossary

arms   guns

artillery   cannons and the troops who fire them

battery   group of cannons and equipment and the soldiers and horses who maintain and transport it all

bayonet   long knife that attaches to the end of a musket or rifle, used in hand to hand combat

brigade   group of up to 5,000 soldiers, usually consisting of 2 to 5 regiments or smaller units, of up to 1,000 men in each

cavalry   soldiers who rode horses

commissioned   appointed by the president to serve in the military

draft   to require men to serve in the military

enlist   to volunteer for military service

fortification   structure built to protect soldiers from an attacking enemy

haversack   large backpack in which soldiers carried food and personal items

infantry   foot soldiers. Members of the infantry are called infantrymen.

ironclad   war ship that had an armor covered top

Medal of Honor   highest military decoration given to members of U.S. armed forces for bravery in combat

militia   small military unit organized by an individual state

minié ball   type of bullet used in a rifle-bored gun or musket, having a cone-shaped base and being longer than the traditional round musket ball

mortar   cannon designed to lob shells over obstacles, used in the Civil War to attack fixed structures rather than soldiers on the battlefield

picket   soldier who guards the outer edges of an army

quartermaster   soldier in charge of giving out supplies to other soldiers

recruit   to get someone to join the military

regiment   group of up to 1,000 soldiers, consisting of up to 10 companies of 100 men in each

rostingyears   corn on the cob

scurvy   disease caused by a lack of Vitamin C

seceded   left the Union

trench   long, deep ditch used by the military for shelter from gunfire and to strengthen defensive positions

Historical Fiction to Read

Alphin, Elaine Marie. *Ghost Cadet*. New York: Scholastic, 1992.
A young boy visiting his grandmother in Virginia makes a friend who is a Civil War ghost.

Beatty, Patricia. *Charley Skedaddle*. New York: Troll Communications, 1989.
The older brother of a twelve-year-old boy is killed in the Battle of Gettysburg. The young boy becomes a drummer for the Union, and then struggles the first time he marches into battle.

Wisler, G. Clifton. *Red Cap*. New York: Penguin Putnam Books for Young Readers, 1994.
A Yankee drummer boy is sent to Andersonville Prison.

Wisler, G. Clifton. *Thunder on the Tennessee*. New York: Penguin Putnam Books for Young Readers, 1995.
A sixteen-year-old boy leaves Texas to fight in the Union Army.

Civil War Places to Visit

Andersonville National Historic Site
496 Cemetery Road
Andersonville, GA 31711
Telephone: 229-924-0343
The park consists of the historic prison site and the National Cemetery with a purpose of providing an understanding of the overall prisoner of war story of the Civil War, to interpret the role of prisoner of war camps in history, and to honor Americans who lost their lives in such camps.

Arlington House/The Robert E. Lee Memorial
George Washington Memorial Parkway
Turkey Run Park
McLean, VA 22101
Telephone: 703-557-0613
Arlington House provides a detailed look at Robert E. Lee's life before and after the Civil War. Here, in 1861, General Lee wrote the letter resigning his commission from the U.S. Army to fight for his native Virginia. The house is restored with many furnishings that were originally owned by Lee's family.

The Civil War Soldiers Museum
108 South Palafox Place
Pensacola, FL 32501
Telephone: 850-469-1900
This museum provides an in-depth trip back to the Civil War through a large collection of artifacts, uniforms, equipment, weapons, art, and life-sized camp scenes. The exhibits include one of the nation's largest displays of Civil War medical artifacts, and hundreds of personal items used by the common soldier during the war.

U.S. Grant Home State Historic Site
P.O. Box 333, Galena, IL 61036
Telephone: 815-777-3310
This 1860s brick home is furnished and decorated as it was in 1868, when the citizens of Galena presented the house to General Grant. Almost all of the furnishings are original.

Index